CW00375980

Rainbows, Ro
and
Magic Shoots

Starter **ANTHOLOGY**

Compiled by
Elspeth Graham and **Mal Peet**

QUARTER PRIMARY
HAMILTON

OXFORD
UNIVERSITY PRESS

Contents

Stories by significant children's authors

Texts with language play

Information texts

Introduction

Long ago, there was a TV programme called *Doctor Who*. Doctor Who could travel through time. His time machine was called the *Tardis*. It looked just like an ordinary phone-box from the outside, but inside, it was huge.

Books are like that. A book isn't very big, but it can have a whole world inside it. Inside this little book there's a porcupine and some pancakes, a weedy wolf and some weird and wonderful mixes. There are real beans and magic beans. There's a swimming pool in here, and something about that lovely word 'sphere'. There are riddles and rhymes, and somewhere it's raining.

Like most books, this one is bigger than it looks.

We hope you enjoy it.

Mal Peet and Elspeth Graham

Wind Song

LILIAN MOORE

When the wind blows
the quiet things speak.
Some whisper, some clang,
Some creak.

Grasses swish.
Treetops sigh.
Flags slap
and snap at the sky.
Wires on poles
whistle and hum.
Ashcans roll.
Windows drum.

When the wind goes –
suddenly
then,
the quiet things
are quiet again.

There is more about sounds on pages 12 and 50.

6

Leisure Centre, Pleasure Centre

JOHN RICE

You go through plate glass doors
with giant red handles,
into light that's as bright
as a million candles.
The chlorine smells
the whole place steaming,
the kids are yelling
and the kids are screaming.

Watch them
      wave jump
      dive thump
      cartwheel
      free wheel
      look cute
      slip chute
      toe stub
      nose rub
in the leisure centre, pleasure centre.

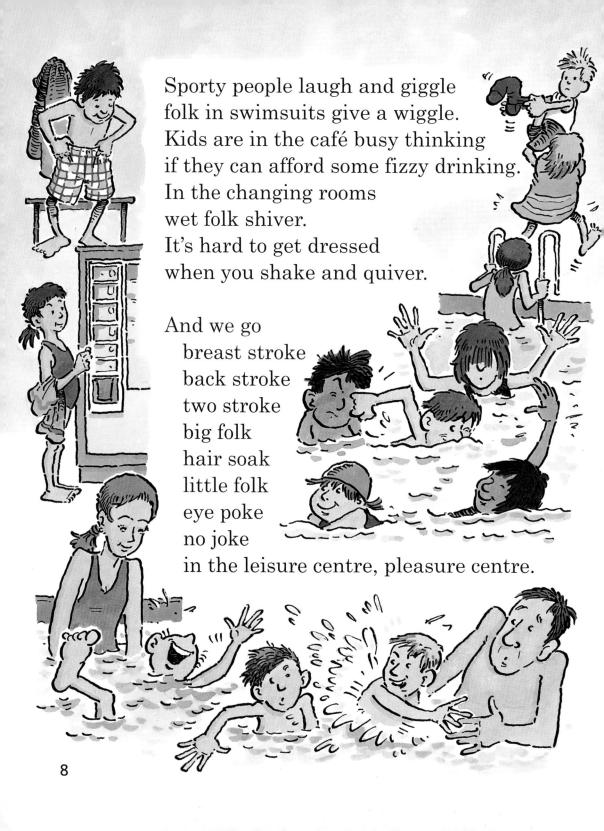

Sporty people laugh and giggle
folk in swimsuits give a wiggle.
Kids are in the café busy thinking
if they can afford some fizzy drinking.
In the changing rooms
wet folk shiver.
It's hard to get dressed
when you shake and quiver.

And we go
   breast stroke
   back stroke
   two stroke
   big folk
   hair soak
   little folk
   eye poke
   no joke
in the leisure centre, pleasure centre.

And now we're driving back home
fish 'n' chips in the car,
eyes are slowly closing
but it's not very far.
Snuggle wuggle up in fresh clean sheets
a leisure centre trip
is the best of treats because you can

    keep fit
    leap sit
    eat crisps
    do twists
    belly flop
    pit stop
    fill up
    with 7-Up
    get going
    blood flowing
    look snappy
    be happy
in the leisure centre, pleasure centre.

Seed

MAL PEET

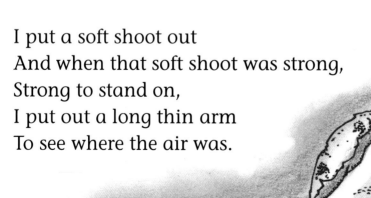

I hid.
I hid in the dark for weeks, I did.

I got fat.
I got fat eating the heat
And drinking the rain.

I got too fat.
I got too fat for my jacket
And my jacket split in two
With a tiny sound like a sneeze, ah-chooooo.

I put a soft shoot out
And when that soft shoot was strong,
Strong to stand on,
I put out a long thin arm
To see where the air was.

The air was not far above my head.
It took just a week to get there.
When I was there I spread
My thin green fingers to the sun
And the sun was pleased to see me.
And I was pleased to see the sun.

And I was pleased to see
So many others just like me,
So many of us reaching up,
Making each hand into a cup
To drink the sun and eat the rain.
I know I'll flower, then I'll die.
And I know we'll all begin again.

There is more about seeds on pages 14, 32, 33 and 60.

The Sound Collector

ROGER MCGOUGH

A stranger called this morning
Dressed all in black and grey
Put every sound into a bag
And carried them away

The whistling of the kettle
The turning of the lock
The purring of the kitten
The ticking of the clock

The popping of the toaster
The crunching of the flakes
When you spread the marmalade
The scraping noise it makes

The hissing of the frying-pan
The ticking of the grill
The bubbling of the bathtub
As it starts to fill

The drumming of the raindrops
On the window-pane
When you do the washing-up
The gurgle of the drain

The crying of the baby
The squeaking of the chair
The swishing of the curtain
The creaking of the stair

A stranger called this morning
He didn't leave his name
Left us only silence
Life will never be the same.

 There is more about sounds on pages 6 and 50.

The Grandad Tree

Trish Cooke

There is a tree at the bottom of Leigh's garden.
An apple tree. Vin, Leigh's big brother, said it
started as a seed and then grew and grew. And
Vin said that tree, where they used to play with
Grandad, that apple tree will be there … for ever.

Their grandad was a baby once and he grew
and grew. Vin said Grandad went to school and
he climbed *coconut* trees, and looked out at the
sea from the top.

And when he was a man he was a husband for
their gran and a dad for their mam and Auntie
Melissa and Uncle Victor and then a grandad for
them.

"That's life," their grandad used to say.

In the spring the apple tree is covered in white blossom.
In summer the apples grow.
In the autumn the leaves fall off.
In the winter it is covered in snow.
And sometimes things die, like trees, like people … like
Grandad. But they don't go away for ever. They stay …
because we remember.

Leigh planted a seed for Grandad, just beside the
apple tree. And when she is sad Vin takes her hand,
and he waters the seed with Leigh.

And it will grow and grow and it will go
through changes
and they'll love it for ever and ever …
just like they'll
always love
Grandad.

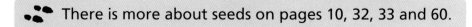 There is more about seeds on pages 10, 32, 33 and 60.

Leon and Bob

Simon James

Leon had moved into town with his mum.
His dad was away in the army.
Leon shared his room with his new friend, Bob.

No one else could see Bob but Leon knew he
was there.
Leon always laid a place for Bob at the table.
"More milk, Bob?" Leon said.

Sometimes Leon's mum couldn't take Leon to
school, but Leon didn't mind.
He always walked to school with Bob.
He always had Bob to talk to.

Often when Leon got home,
there was a letter waiting
for him from his dad.
Bob liked to hear Leon read
it over and over again.

One Saturday, Leon
heard some noises in
the street below.
He saw a new family
moving in next door.
A boy looked up at Leon
and waved.
Leon waved back.

That night Leon kept thinking about the boy
next door.
He decided to go round there in the morning.
'But you'll have to come with me, Bob,' he said.

The next day Leon and Bob ate their breakfast
very quickly.
Then Leon grabbed his ball and rushed outside.

Leon ran up the steps of
next-door's house.
He was about halfway
when suddenly he
realised Bob wasn't
there any more.

Leon sat down.
He was all alone.
He could ring the bell or he could go home.
Why wasn't Bob there to help him?

Leon rang the bell and waited.
The door opened.
"Hello," said the boy.
"H-hello," said Leon. "Would you like
to go to the park?"

"OK," said the boy. "I'm
just going to the park,
Mum," he called.
Together Leon and the boy
walked down the steps
towards the street.
"My name's Leon," said
Leon. "What's yours?"

"Bob," said Bob.

I Don't Want to **Clean my Teeth**

Bel Mooney

Once there was a little girl called Kitty who didn't want to clean her teeth. Each night she would cry and scream and throw her toothbrush to the ground. One night she even wrote her name in toothpaste on the bathroom wall. "I *won't* clean my teeth," she said.

Kitty's mum was cross. "If you don't clean your teeth they will all fall out," she said.

"I don't care," said Kitty. "I want to have a mouth with no teeth in it, just like Grandad's."

"How will you be able to chew your food?" asked Mum.

"I will only eat soup and Instant Whip and porridge," said Kitty, "because they don't need any chewing!"

That night Kitty went to bed without cleaning her teeth. She put her finger in her mouth and tried to get out a piece of meat that was stuck in her tooth. It always made Mum angry when she did that. Kitty could still taste the sugar on the apple pie she had for pudding, and the delicious chocolatey taste of the cocoa.

"Yum, yum," she said. "I like to taste my tea. When you clean your teeth all the time you can only taste boring old toothpaste. I don't believe all the things the grown-ups tell you about sweets making your teeth fall out – and anyway, I don't CARE!"

And Kitty took a sweet from the packet she had hidden under her pillow, and chewed it happily. Then she turned over and fell asleep.

Kitty started to dream. She dreamt that she was walking in a huge, dark wood, where the trees grew thickly and no birds sang.

Suddenly she heard a loud cry. She ran towards the sound, and there in a clearing she saw little Red Riding Hood with the wolf. But it wasn't Little Red Riding Hood who was crying, it was the wolf!

Red Riding Hood kicked the wolf sharply on his knee and laughed. "I'm not afraid of you any more, because you're just a silly old toothless has-been," she shouted.

The wolf turned to Kitty and she saw that it was true. He had no teeth. "Where are your teeth?" Kitty asked. "They all fell out," the wolf sighed.

There is more about Little Red Riding Hood on pages 36 and 52.

Milly

PIPPA GOODHART

> Alice and her grandad are making pancakes.

"Sift the flour well," said Grandad. "We don't want lumpy pancakes!"

Alice held the sieve over a bowl with one hand and spooned flour into it with the other. Her nose itched, but there were no hands left to scratch her nose with so she just wrinkled it and tried to ignore the tickle. Catkin tried to catch the handle of the spoon as Alice stirred. Some of the flour flicked onto Catkin's grey fur. It made her look like a ghostly old cat. Alice laughed.

"You concentrate!' said
Grandad. He handed her a
wire whisk and slowly
began to pour a mixture
of egg and milk in a river
down the side of Alice's
flour mountain. "Now
whisk away! These have
got to be the finest
pancakes ever!"
Alice held the bowl still and whisked
until her arm ached while Grandad
poured. Gradually the dry flour and the wet
eggy milk came together to make a thick
sloppy batter.

"Do you know something, Alice?" asked
Grandad. "Did you know that you can give a
hundred people the same flour, eggs and milk and
yet the pancakes they make with those ingredients
would all turn out quite differently?"

"How do you mean?" Alice itched her nose
with the back of her hand.

"Well," said Grandad. "Some folks would make
their pancakes thick, some thin, some crisp, some

soggy. Smooth or lumpy, big or small, they'd all
be different. People are like pancakes."

Alice laughed.

"It's true!" said Grandad. "Children can grow
up with the same parents, in the same home and
with the same chances, and yet they will all turn
out quite different! There's another way that
pancakes are like children too. They both need
plenty of rest! We'll leave this mixture to rest in
the bowl while we lay the table for our feast."

There is more about pancakes on pages 26 and 84.

A Recipe for Grandad's Pancakes

This recipe will make about 10 pancakes.

You will need
- 125 g plain flour
- a pinch of salt
- 1 egg
- 300 ml milk
- a little oil

Note
Always ask an adult
to help you cook.

Method
1 Sift the flour into a mixing
   bowl. Add the salt, then make
   a dip in the flour with a spoon.

2 Crack the egg into the milk.
   Whisk for a few seconds.

3 Tip some of the eggy milk into the
   dip in the flour and begin to mix.

4 Slowly add the rest of the eggy milk
   and beat until all the flour is mixed in.

5 Whisk to make a smooth, sloppy batter. There should be tiny bubbles on its surface.

6 Leave the batter to rest for half an hour.

7 Heat a little oil in a frying pan until hot, then add a spoonful of batter.

8 Tilt the pan to spread the batter. When bubbles form on the surface of the pancake it is time to flip it over. Cook until both sides are golden brown.

Eat with a sprinkle of sugar and a good squeeze of lemon juice.

 There is more about pancakes on pages 23 and 84.

Farlock Park: A Fun Day Out For All The Family

Key
1 Shop and displays
2 Café
3 Ice creams
4 Pets' centre
5 Adventure playground
6 Picnic area
7 Ostrich paddock
8 Red deer paddock
9 Go-karts
10 Steam engines

Car park

Entrance

Bus park

29

Get into Shape with Yoga

ELSPETH GRAHAM

THE STORK is a yoga position. It is good for your balance. It keeps your spine straight and it helps make your legs stronger.

- Stand upright with your legs and feet together. Breathe in.

- Breathe out. Pull your left foot up behind you and hold it with your left hand. Hold it close to your body.

- Breathe in and lift your right arm up above your head. Breathe out. Stay in this position and try not to wobble. Now breathe normally for a minute or so. Relax.

- Repeat the position using your right foot and left arm.

Newspaper Trees

How to make a tall tree out of old newspapers

You will need: 4 sheets of newspaper, sticky tape, scissors

1 Lay out the sheets of newspaper, flat and on top of each other. Now move the top two sheets to one side.
2 Roll the paper into a tube and then fix it with sticky tape.
3 Next, cut three long slits in the tube, starting from the same end each time.
4 Now pull the middle of the tube up and out. Your tree will grow and spread its branches!

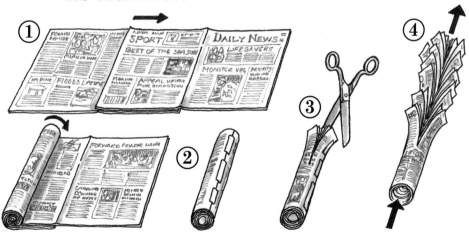

Sow and Grow

Web's
50p
fun seeds

Jack's Giant
Runner Beans
Scarlet Emperor

Sow and Grow
with Mum or Dad!

JAN	
FEB	
MAR	
APR	
MAY	
JUN	
JUL	
AUG	
SEP	
OCT	
NOV	
DEC	

When to sow:
- In pots indoors in April
- Outdoors from May to June
- Sow 5 cm deep and 25 cm apart.

Did you know?
Runner beans need something to climb up. Use:

- a net

- a bamboo wigwam.

Sow the seeds
Pick the beans

Guaranteed to grow!

There is more about seeds on pages 10, 14, 33 and 60.

Jack and the Beanstalk

RETOLD BY MAL PEET

Once upon a time, in a poor little cottage, a boy called Jack lived with his mother. They were as poor as poor can be. All they had was their cow, Milky White. One day Jack's mother sighed and said "We'll have to sell Milky White. Take her to the town and sell her, Jack."

Sadly Jack set out for the town with the cow. Before he got there, a strange little man stopped him.

"I'd like to buy your cow," he said. "I'll give you these for her."

He held out his hand. There were five red beans in it.

Jack laughed. "You must be joking," he said.

"Oh no," said the little man, "not at all. These are magic beans. If you plant them tonight they will grow up to the sky before the morning. They'll make you very, very rich."

There are two things you need to know about Jack. One is that he was not very clever. The other is that he was very, very, fed up with being poor. The word "rich" worked on him like a magic spell.

He sold Milky White to the little man for five red beans.

When Jack came home with five red beans and no cow, his mother was not pleased. She screamed. She threw the beans into the garden and screamed again. Then she sat and wept.

Jack crept off to his bedroom. Soon he fell asleep.

In the morning when he woke up, his mouth fell open and his eyes bulged. Right outside his window was a huge tree. It had five thick green trunks twisted around each other, and leaves as big as the roof. And it hadn't been there the day before. Jack leaned out of the window and looked up. The top of the tree was lost in the clouds.

"The beans!" he gasped. "They *were* magic! That's not a tree, it's a giant beanstalk!"

He couldn't stop himself. He stepped right out of the window and onto a thick green branch. He started to climb. It was easy. And once he had started, he couldn't stop.

There is more about seeds on pages 10, 14, 32 and 60.

Little Red Riding Wolf

LAURENCE ANHOLT

In the very darkest corner of the deep dark wood sat the Big Bad Girl.

The Big Bad Girl was just about as BIG and BAD as a girl can be, and all the woodland animals were afraid of her.

She hung about beside the forest path and carved her name on trees. She shouted rude things at any little animal who passed by.

36

The Big Bad Girl tripped up little deer. She stole
fir cones from baby squirrels and threw them at the
poor little hedgehogs. The woodland birds didn't
dare to sing when the Big Bad Girl was around!

But the person the Big Bad Girl liked to tease
most of all was a charming little wolf cub who
often passed by on his way to visit his dear
old granny wolf.

Little Wolfie was the sweetest, fluffiest, politest little cub you could ever hope to meet. He would run along the path, *skippety-skip*, carrying a basket of freshly baked goodies for Old Granny Wolf, singing all the time …

I'm a little wolfie, good and sweet.
I am tidy, I am neat.
With a basket full of lovely grub,
I am Granny's favourite cub.

"Wot's in yer basket today, Little-Weedy-Wolfie-Wimp?" snarled the Big Bad Girl. "Mmmm, apple pies? I'll take those. Jam sandwiches? Very tasty."

"Oh dear, oh dear! Now there will be nothing for dear Old Granny Wolf," wailed Little Wolfie. And his little wolfie tears rolled into the empty basket.

There is more about Little Red Riding Hood on pages 19 and 52.

Sitti's Secrets

NAOMI SHIHAB NYE

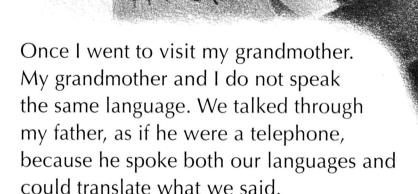

Once I went to visit my grandmother.
My grandmother and I do not speak
the same language. We talked through
my father, as if he were a telephone,
because he spoke both our languages and
could translate what we said.

I called her *Sitti*, which means Grandma
in Arabic. She called me *habibi*, which
means darling. Her voice danced as high as the
whistles of birds. Her voice giggled and
whooshed like a wind going around corners. She
had a thousand rivers in her voice.

A few curls of dark hair peeked out of her scarf on one side, and a white curl peeked out on the other side. I wanted her to take off the scarf so I could see if her hair was striped.

Soon we had invented our own language together. Sitti pointed at my stomach to ask if I was hungry. I pointed to the door to ask if she wanted to go outside. We walked to the fields to watch men picking lentils. We admired the sky with hums and claps. We crossed the road to buy milk from a family that kept one spotted cow. I called the cow *habibi,* and it winked at me. We thanked the cow, with whistles and clicks, for the fresh milk that we carried home in Sitti's little teapot.

Every day I played with my cousins, Fowzi, Sami, Hani, and Hendia from next door. We played marbles together in their courtyard. Their marbles were blue and green and spun through the dust like planets. We didn't need words to play marbles.

My grandmother lives on the other side of the earth. She eats cucumber for breakfast, with yoghurt and bread. She bakes the big, flat bread in a round, old oven next to her house. A fire burns in the middle. She pats the dough between her hands and presses it out to bake on a flat black rock in the centre of the oven. My father says she has been baking that bread for a hundred years.

Why Bear has a Stumpy Tail

A story from Norway

RETOLD BY ANN PILLING

One day, Bear met Fox. Fox was slinking along as usual, his mouth stuffed with fish.

"Where did you get those fish?" said Bear. It was winter and food was hard to find. He was extremely hungry. He had never tried catching a fish but he was determined to learn. A few fat fish would make him a tasty meal.

"It's very easy," Fox told him. But he didn't like Bear very much and he decided to play a trick on him. "All you do is find a lake and slide across the ice till you reach the middle. You cut a hole and you sit down, and you stick your tail into the water.

It stings a bit but you must leave it there as long as you can, because when it stings the fish will start biting. They're curious creatures, they'll soon come up to see what's happening.

The longer you can stay there the more fish you'll catch. They'll hang on to your tail. When you've caught some you just give it a little twist and out they come. Got it?"

"Got it," said Bear and he shambled off to find a lake. It sounded very easy. His mouth was watering as he banged at the ice with his huge furry paws and he'd soon made a nice big hole. Sitting on the edge, he stuck in his lovely long tail and waited.

Just how long he sat there Bear could never say. He grew so cold his rear end went quite numb. As for his tail, he couldn't feel it at all and there was no way of telling if he'd caught any fish. He got tired in the end, and stood up in a huff.

Snap! Bear peered down at the frozen lake. No fish. No tail either. It had frozen solid and broken right off. All he had left was a funny little stump.

The Shepherd Boy at School

A story from Ethiopia

RETOLD BY ELIZABETH LAIRD

Once, there was a shepherd boy who started going to school. He found his lessons very difficult, and the hardest one of all was Maths.

"Take 3 from 5," the teacher said. "What's the answer?"

The boy shook his head.

"What's 4 minus 2?" asked the teacher. "You must be able to do that one."

But the boy couldn't.

"Well," the teacher said. "Here's an example you ought to understand. Say you have five sheep in your fold and one of them runs out through a hole in the fence. How many will you have left?"

"That's easy," the shepherd boy answered. "I won't have any left."

"How can you be so stupid?" answered the teacher.

"I'm not stupid!" said the boy. "I don't know much about Maths, but I know all about sheep. If one goes out through a hole in the fence, all the others will follow!"

5−1=?

Minnie

A rhyme from the USA

ANON.

I went downtown
To meet Mrs Brown.
She gave me a nickel
To buy me a pickle.
The pickle was sour
She gave me a flower
The flower was dead
She gave me a thread
The thread was thin
She gave me a pin
The pin was sharp
She gave me a harp
The harp began to sing
Minnie and a minnie and a ha, ha, ha.
Minnie and a minnie and a ha, ha, ha,
Kissed her fellow in a trolley car.
I told Ma, Ma told Pa.
Minnie got a spanking and a ha, ha, ha.

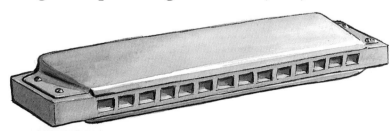

My Sari

DEBJANI CHATTERJEE

Saris hang on the washing line:
a rainbow in our neighbourhood.
This little orange one is mine,
it has a mango leaf design.
I wear it as a Rani would.
It wraps around me like sunshine,
it ripples silky down my spine,
and I stand tall and feel so good.

Praise Song of the Wind

TRADITIONAL POEM OF THE TELEUT PEOPLE OF SIBERIA
ANON.

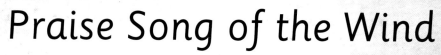

Trees with weak roots
I will strike, I the wind.
I will roar, I will whistle.

Haycocks built today
I will scatter, I the wind.
I will roar, I will whistle.

Badly made haycocks
I will carry off, I the wind.
I will roar, I will whistle.

Uncovered stacks of sheaves
I will soak through, I the wind.
I will roar, I will whistle.

Houses not tightly roofed
I will destroy, I the wind.
I will roar, I will whistle.

Hay piled in sheds
I will tear apart, I the wind.
I will roar, I will whistle.

Fire kindled in the road
I will set flickering, I the wind.
I will roar, I will whistle.

Houses with bad smoke-holes
I will shake, I the wind.
I will roar, I will whistle.

The farmer who does not think
I will make to think, I the wind.
I will roar, I will whistle.

The worthless slug-a-bed
I will wake, I the wind.
I will roar, I will whistle.

There is more about sounds on pages 6 and 12.

Little Red Rap

TONY MITTON

Just on the edge
of a deep, dark wood
lived a girl called
Little Red Riding Hood.
Her grandmother lived
not far away,
so Red went to pay her
a visit one day.

She took some cake
and she took some wine
packed in a basket
nice and fine.

And her ma said, "Red,
now just watch out,
for they say that
Big Bad Wolf's about."

But Red went off
with a hop and a skip.
She was feeling good,
she was feeling hip.
So she took her time,
she picked some flowers,
and soon the minutes
had grown to hours.

And the Big Bad Wolf,
who knew her plan,
he turned his nose
and he ran and ran.
He ran till he came
to her grandmother's door.
Then he locked her up
with a great big roar.

He took her place
in her nice warm bed,
and he waited there
for Little Miss Red.
So when Little Red,
she stepped inside,
that wolf, his eyes
went open wide.

Says Red, "Why Gran,
what great big eyes!"
Says Wolf, "I'm trying
you out for size."

Says Red, "Why, Gran,
you're covered in hair!"
Says Wolf, "Now, dear,
it's rude to stare."

And goodness, Gran,
what a great big grin!"
Says Wolf, "All the better
to fit you in!"

But Little Miss Red
says, "Not so fast …"
and she calls to a woodcutter
strolling past.
"Hey, you there, John!
Can I borrow your axe?"
And she gave that Wolfie
three good whacks.

That wolf ran off
with a holler and a shout
and Little Miss Red
let Grandma out.

They called the woodcutter
in to dine
and they all sat down
to the cake and the wine.

And that's how the story ends –
Just fine!

There is more about Little Red Riding Hood on
pages 19 and 36.

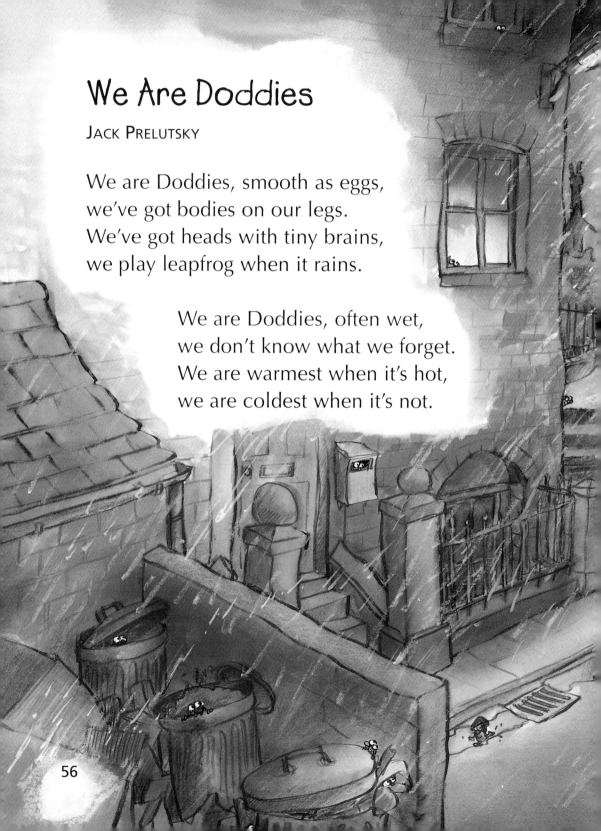

We Are Doddies

JACK PRELUTSKY

We are Doddies, smooth as eggs,
we've got bodies on our legs.
We've got heads with tiny brains,
we play leapfrog when it rains.

We are Doddies, often wet,
we don't know what we forget.
We are warmest when it's hot,
we are coldest when it's not.

We are Doddies, small and round,
we're not missing when we're found.
We are closest when we're near,
we're not there when we are here.

We are Doddies, we don't mind
if we leave ourselves behind.
So we never make a fuss,
we are Doddies, look for us.

My First Oxford Dictionary

COMPILED BY EVELYN GOLDSMITH

dictionary (dictionaries)
A dictionary is a book
where you can find out
what a word means and
how to spell it.

die (dying, died)
When someone or
something dies, they stop
living.
Plants die without water.

different
If something is different
from something else, it is
not like it in some way.
*Our pens are different. Mine is red
and yours is blue.*

difficult
Difficult things are not easy
to do.
This is a difficult tree to climb.

dig (digging, dug)
To dig means to move soil
away to make a hole in the
ground.

*The dog dug a hole to bury his
bone.*

dinner (dinners)
Dinner is the main meal of
the day.

dinosaur (dinosaurs)
A dinosaur is a large reptile
that lived millions of years
ago.
See **Dinosaurs** on page 123.

direction (directions)
1 A direction is the way you
go to get somewhere.
The school is in that direction.
2 Directions are words or
pictures that tell you what
to do.
Read the directions on the bottle.

dirt
Dirt is dust or mud.
Wash that dirt off your knees.

dirty (dirtier, dirtiest)
Something that is dirty is covered with mud, food, or other marks.

My clothes always get dirty when I play football.

disappear (disappearing, disappeared)
If something disappears, you cannot see it any longer.
After two days, my spots disappeared.

disappointed
If someone is disappointed, they feel sad because something they were hoping for did not happen.
Jessica was disappointed when her best friend could not come to her party.

disaster (disasters)
A disaster is something very bad that happens suddenly.
The storm was a disaster. Thousands of trees were blown down.

discover (discovering, discovered)
When you discover something, you find out about it.
I've discovered a secret drawer.

discuss (discussing, discussed)
When people discuss things, they talk about them.
We discussed the best way to build the tree house.

dish (dishes)
1 A dish is for cooking or serving food.
2 The dishes are all the things that have to be washed up after a meal.

Beans and More Beans

ELSPETH GRAHAM

When a bean seed is put into damp soil it can begin to grow.

First, the seed takes in water and swells so much that its hard skin splits open and a tiny root grows out.

Next, a shoot begins to grow. The shoot grows upwards and the root grows downwards.

After a few days, the shoot will push up through the soil and into the sunlight.

The bean pods grow bigger and bigger. Inside each pod there are new beans. Each bean could grow into a new bean plant.

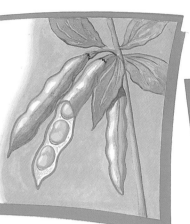

Later, the plant begins to flower. When the flowers die, tiny bean pods may start to grow inside them.

The sunlight helps the plant grow taller and stronger. The plant grows lots of leaves.

 There is more about seeds on pages 10, 14, 32 and 33.

The Rain Cycle

Rain comes from clouds, but where do clouds
come from? Where does all the rainwater go?
These two pages explain the rain cycle.

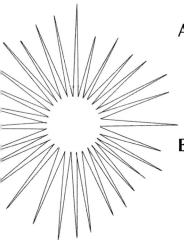

A The sun warms water. Some of the water
evaporates. It turns into a gas called
water vapour. Water vapour rises into
the air.

B The air is cold up in the sky. The water
vapour cools and becomes tiny droplets
of water. They collect together to make
clouds.

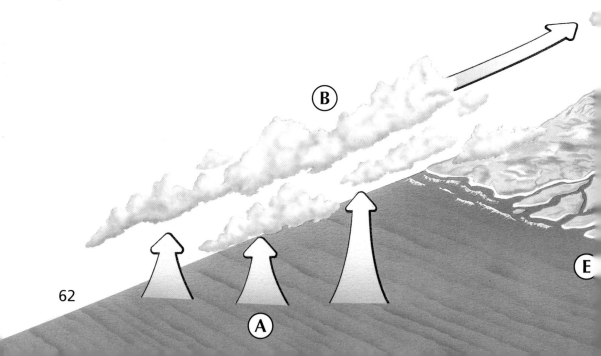

C The water droplets get too big and heavy to float in the air. They fall to the ground as rain.

D Rainwater collects in streams and rivers, and the streams and rivers flow into the sea or lakes.

E Then the rain cycle starts all over again.

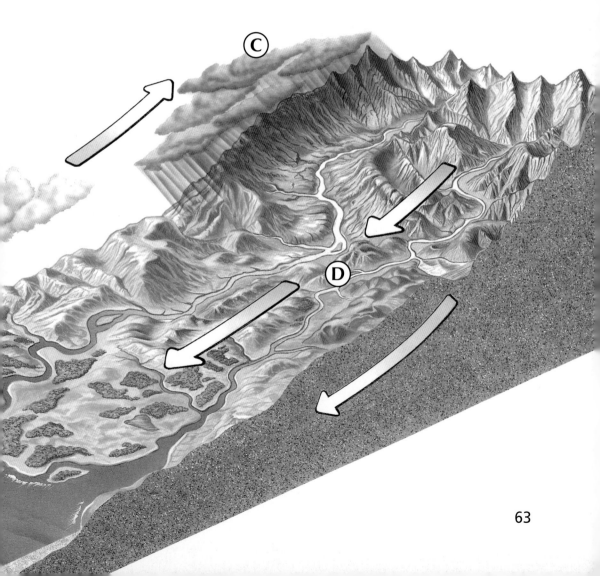

The Apple Child

VIVIAN FRENCH

There was once a cold village on the side of
a tall cold mountain. Behind the village was a
stony field where a flock of thin sheep huddled
together under the shadow of a few spindly
apple trees, and high above the mountain hung
the moon; a pale cold moon that sent long dark
shadows sprawling along the ground, creeping
in and out of the village, and crouching down
beside Ben's small cold cottage.

"*Brrrr,*" shivered Ben, pulling an old sack
around his shoulders. A little fire flickered in the
grate, but there was no more wood left in the
broken basket by the chimney. He got up and
stared out of the window. Up on the
mountainside he could see the apple trees
quivering in the wind.

"I'll run up and see if there are any twigs or sticks under the trees," said Ben. He wrapped the sack more closely about himself, and slipped out of the cottage and up the street. The wind caught him and tugged and pulled at him, but he put his head down and trudged on to where the cold field lay beyond the last house.

The sheep shifted unwillingly as Ben walked among them; "Saaaad," they bleated, "saaad!" The trees were moaning and muttering to each other, the wind snapped at their branches and whipped their last few leaves off and away.

High in the sky the moon gazed down. Ben
glanced up, and for a moment thought he saw a
watching silver face.

"What can I do, Moon?" he called. "I'm cold –
I'm ever so cold!"

There was no answer from the moon, but the
wind suddenly dropped. Just for a moment there
was a stillness, a silence as if all the moonlit
world was holding its breath. Only a moment it
lasted, and then up sprang the wind with a howl
and a shriek, and tore the sack from his back. The
trees bent and swayed, and with a loud crash a
long branch fell to the ground beside him.

"Thank you! Thank you!" Ben shouted,
and he picked up the branch and ran as fast
as he could back to his small cold cottage.

The fire was a mere glimmer, but as he fed it first the smallest twig and then the bigger ones, it began to take heart and to glow warmly. Breaking the branch, he built the fire up higher, until the shadows were dancing and the smell of apple wood filled the room.

"*Oh!*" Ben stared as the flames sparkled and crackled and burnt red and green and silver.

CRACK! A log of the apple wood split into two halves, and a small green child no bigger than Ben's hand stepped out of the fire and on to the floor beside him.

"Good evening," said the child.

Hedgehogs Don't Eat Hamburgers

Vivian French

Four little hedgehogs called Hector, Hattie, Harry and
Hester fancy hamburgers to eat. Sly Fox offers to show
them the way.

Hector and Hattie and Harry and Hester set off
after Fox.

"Here we go, here we go, here we go," they
sang as they walked along.

"SSSHHH!" said Fox.

"Oh," said Hector and Hattie and Harry
and Hester.

They walked up the hill and down the hill.

"Are we nearly there?" asked Hector.

"Nearly," said Fox. He sniffed the air.
"Yes, we're nearly there."

Hector sniffed the air too.

"What is it?" he asked.

"That's the smell of the town," said Fox.
"That's where the hamburgers are."

"Oh," said Hector. He sniffed the air again. He could smell cars, and smoke, and shops, and houses. He could smell danger. "Maybe I don't want a hamburger today. Maybe I'll have big black beetles, or slow slimy slugs, or fine fat snails. Maybe hedgehogs don't eat hamburgers after all."

Hector turned around, and Hattie and Harry and Hester all turned around too.

"Here we go, here we go, here we go!" they sang.

"JUST A MINUTE," said Fox, and he opened his mouth wide. His teeth were sharp and white. "What about MY tea?"

"YOU can have a hamburger," said Hector.

"But I don't WANT a hamburger," said Fox. "I want little fat HEDGEHOGS!" And he jumped at Hector and Hattie and Harry and Hester.

"HERE WE GO, HERE WE GO, HERE WE GO," sang all four little hedgehogs, and they rolled themselves up tightly into four prickly balls.

"OWWWW!" said Fox as he hurt his nose. "OW! OW! OW!" He turned round and ran up the hill and down the hill. He didn't stop running until he got home to his mummy.

There is more about hedgehogs on page 94.

Banger

DICK KING-SMITH

Steven did love sausages!

To say that they were his favourite food was not enough. Steven had sausages all the time. He had them for breakfast, lunch, tea and supper. He had big sausages, short fat ones and long thin ones, pork sausages, beef sausages, Cumberland sausages, chipolatas, saveloys, salami and frankfurters.

What, no cheese?

He ate them fried, boiled, baked, grilled or smoked, hot or cold. And it wasn't simply that Steven had sausages for every meal, every day of every week of every year – oh no, it was more than that. He had sausages with everything he ate.

At breakfast time he would put cornflakes and sugar and milk on a sausage, then eat a sausage with bacon and eggs, and then slice a sausage down the middle and spread each half with butter and jam.

You can guess what Steven always began with at lunch and at supper, but for afters he might have rice pudding and sausage, sausage and custard, sausage dumplings with treacle, or perhaps best of all, a vanilla ice-cream cornet with a sausage stuck in the top of it. As for tea, well there were always sausages on hot buttered toast, and perhaps chocolate éclairs with a sausage on each, or just simply sausage-meat sandwiches. And of course Steven never stirred his tea with a spoon if there was a sausage handy.

George's Marvellous Medicine

ROALD DAHL

> George's grandma is a witchy, crabby old thing.
> George makes her a "medicine" out of all sorts of
> horrible stuff. She swallows some.

Then a funny thing happened.
Grandma's body gave a sudden
sharp twist and a sudden sharp
jerk and she flipped herself clear
out of the chair and landed neatly
on her two feet on the carpet.

"That's terrific, Grandma!"
George cried. "You haven't stood up like that for
years! Look at you! You're standing up all on your
own and you're not even using a stick!"

Grandma didn't even hear him. The frozen
pop-eyed look was back with her again now.
She was miles away in another world.

Marvellous medicine, George told himself.
He found it fascinating to stand there watching
what it was doing to the old hag. What next?
he wondered.

He soon found out.

Suddenly she began to grow.

It was quite slow at first … just a very gradual inching upwards … up, up, up … inch by inch … getting taller and taller … about an inch every few seconds … and in the beginning George didn't notice it.

But when she had passed the five foot six mark and was going on up towards being six feet tall, George gave a jump and shouted, "Hey, Grandma! You're *growing*! You're *going up*! Hang on, Grandma! You'd better stop now or you'll be hitting the ceiling!"

But Grandma didn't stop.

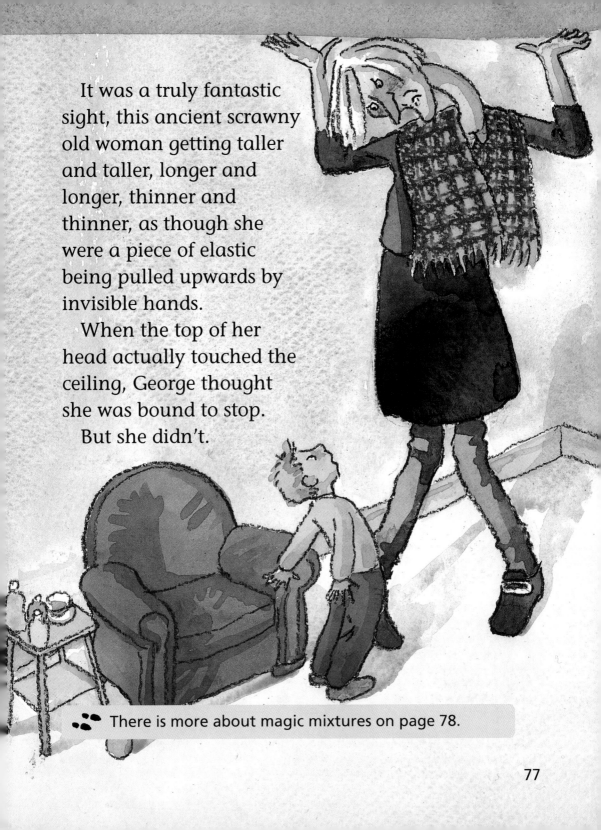

It was a truly fantastic sight, this ancient scrawny old woman getting taller and taller, longer and longer, thinner and thinner, as though she were a piece of elastic being pulled upwards by invisible hands.

When the top of her head actually touched the ceiling, George thought she was bound to stop.

But she didn't.

There is more about magic mixtures on page 78.

Dixxer's Excellent Elixir

JACK PRELUTSKY

Dexter Dixxer mixed elixir
in his quick elixir mixer.
"It's an excellent elixir,"
Dexter boasted, "very fine
for afflictions which assail you,
aches which irritate and ail you,
guaranteed to rarely fail you,
only nineteen ninety-nine!"

His elixir tasted icky,
it was fishy, squishy, sticky,
just to swallow it was tricky,
and I tried to spit it out.
But too late! My tongue already
started turning to spaghetti,
and my hair was red confetti
with a touch of sauerkraut.

I grew feathers on my belly,
all my fingers felt like jelly,
then my feet got really smelly,
and my ears were green as limes.
I was squawking, I was squealing,
and I had a sinking feeling,
so I jumped up to the ceiling,
and I sneezed eleven times.

I was yipping, I was yapping,
as my kneecaps started clapping,
then my earlobes started flapping,
and my nose turned violet.
So I ran and told my mother,
"This elixir's like no other!"
Now I share it with my brother –
it's the best elixir yet!

There is more about magic mixtures on page 75.

Cat

ELEANOR FARJEON

Cat!
Scat!
Atter her, atter her,
Sleeky flatterer,
Spitfire chatterer,
Scatter her, scatter her,
    Off her mat!
    Wuff!
    Wuff!
    Treat her rough!
Git her, git her,
Whiskery spitter!
Catch her, catch her,
Green-eyed scratcher!
    Slathery
    Slithery
    Hisser,
    Don't miss her!

Run till you're dithery,
　　Hithery
　　Thithery
　　Pfitts! Pfitts!
　　How she spits!
　　Spitch! Spatch!
　　Can't she scratch!

Scritching the bark
Of the sycamore-tree,
She's reached her ark
And's hissing at me
　　Pfitts! Pfitts!
　　Wuff! Wuff!
　　Scat,
　　Cat!
　　That's
　　That!

The Answers

ROBERT CLAIRMONT

"When did the world begin and how?"
I asked a lamb, a goat, a cow.

"What's it all about and why?"
I asked a hog as he went by.

"Where will the whole thing end, and when?"
I asked a duck, a goose, a hen.

And I copied all the answers, too:
A quack, a honk, an oink, a moo.

A Little Alliteration

MIKE JUBB

A little alliteration,
like "lizards licking liquorice",
is a super sound sensation,
so snortsomeful and snickerish.
Children chewing chocolate chips
are standing at the station,
and taking turns to try to teach
a little alliteration.

Untitled

ROGER McGOUGH

To amuse
    emus
on warm summer nights

    Kiwis
do wiwis
from spectacular heights

Betty Botter's Batter

ANON.

Betty Botter bought some butter.
"But," she said, "the butter's bitter.
If I put it in my batter
It will make my batter bitter.
But a bit of better butter,
That would make my batter better."
So she bought a bit of butter
Better than her bitter butter
And she put it in her batter
And the batter was not bitter.
So it was better Betty Botter
Bought a bit of better butter.

There is more about pancakes on pages 23 and 26.

Brian Brownlow

Brian Brownlow bought a big bag
  of bright blue beans.
Did Brian Brownlow buy a big
  bag of bright blue beans?
If Brian Brownlow bought a big
  bag of bright blue beans,
Where's the big bag of bright blue
  beans Brian Brownlow bought?

Sharon Shelley

Sharon Shelley shelled seven shiny shellfish.
Did Sharon Shelley shell seven shiny shellfish?
If Sharon Shelley shelled seven shiny shellfish,
Where are the shells of the seven shiny
  shellfish Sharon Shelley shelled?
(Sharon left them on the sea-shore
  with all the other shells.)

What am I?
Three riddles

MAL PEET

I live in your house.
When you're not here,
I'm quiet as a mouse.
When you're here,
I gather your dreams from the air
and show them to you, square.

I am no wider than your arms
but I can hold a hippo
or a hospital.

We never talk.
You never take me for a walk.
You often laugh at me.
I don't mind.
But sometimes you turn me off.

I am
A big black and white
Jigsaw
Standing in a field.
What am I?

When U C me
U C U in me.
Y?
What must I B?

87

Spheres

PETER PATILLA

WHAT IS A SPHERE?

A **sphere** is a perfectly round ball. The distance from the centre of the sphere to anywhere on its surface is always the same.

A SPINNING CIRCLE

Spin a coin on a table top and you will see a sphere shape. A circle spinning around its diameter makes a sphere.

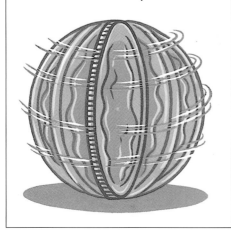

A sphere can be solid or hollow. It is very strong and can stand powerful forces pressing in on it.

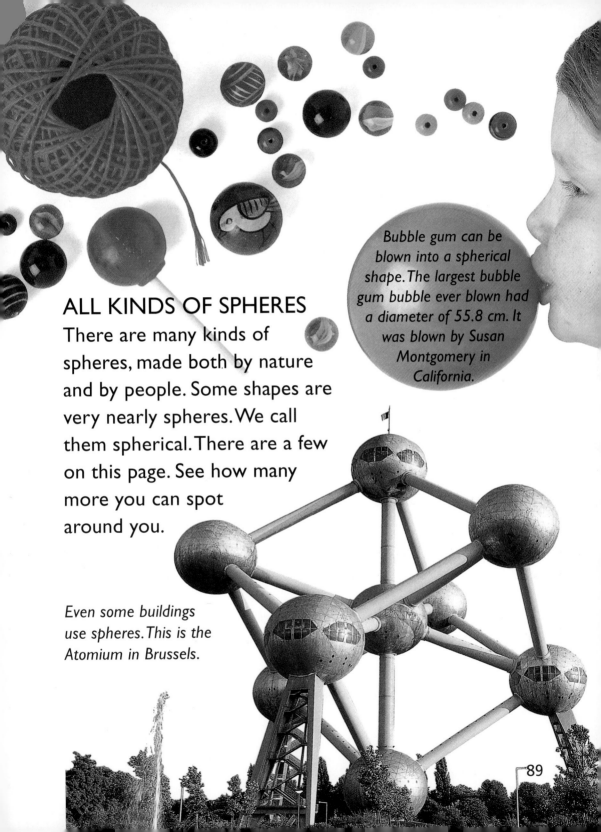

ALL KINDS OF SPHERES

There are many kinds of spheres, made both by nature and by people. Some shapes are very nearly spheres. We call them spherical. There are a few on this page. See how many more you can spot around you.

Bubble gum can be blown into a spherical shape. The largest bubble gum bubble ever blown had a diameter of 55.8 cm. It was blown by Susan Montgomery in California.

Even some buildings use spheres. This is the Atomium in Brussels.

About Vivian French

Vivian French was an actor and wrote plays before she started writing stories for children. Her first three stories were published in 1990. Since then she has written more than a hundred books, both fiction and non-fiction. She loves visiting schools to tell stories and to read from her books. Vivian has four daughters. She lives in Bristol.

This is an extract from an interview:

Interviewer What made you want to become a writer?

Vivian French I didn't. I never thought of being a writer when I was at school. I wasn't very good at writing or spelling – one of my teachers tore up one of my stories in front of the whole class. I wanted to be a long-distance lorry driver, or to drive steam trains, or be an actor.

Some of Vivian French's non-fiction books are:

The Apple Trees   *Caterpillar Caterpillar*
Spider Watching   *Growing Frogs*

These are all published by Walker Books.

This is a message to readers of this book from Vivian French:

I love words. I've always talked a lot – my excuse is that I'm practising using words. The best ones feel good in your mouth every time you say them. Try saying *clock, clock, clock, clock* … doesn't it sound exactly like a clock ticking?

When I write a story I always read it aloud over and over to make sure that it sounds right. The best words are like music; they can make you feel better, or angry, or very sad. I loved being read to when I was little (I was not very good at reading to myself) and I often used to end up in floods of tears … but that's the power of stories. When people ask me for useful tips on writing I always say *Read your words out loud!*

Animal Armour

Elspeth Graham

When faced with danger, many animals run away
or hide. Some animals do not run away because
they have special body armour to protect them.

Some have strong shells, some have scales, some
have prickles, and some can roll into balls.

Shells

Lots of sea animals have strong shells.

Some crabs have separate hard plates that are
fixed together by moving joints. They also have
large powerful claws.

hard shell

head pulled inside shell

Tortoises have very hard body shells. A tortoise can pull its head inside its shell and tightly fold up its legs.

Scales

Pangolins have armour that is made up of lots of separate plates or scales. These scales cover the pangolin's head, back and tail.

A pangolin can also roll up into a ball. Its head is tucked away in the middle of the ball.

scales

head

tail

Prickles

Hedgehogs are covered in prickles, or spines. The spines are very sharp and if a hedgehog is threatened it makes its spines stand on end. At the same time the hedgehog curls up into a tight ball.

Porcupines are also covered in sharp spines or quills. If a porcupine is threatened by an enemy it gives a warning. It stamps its feet and rattles its quills. If the other animal ignores this warning, the porcupine charges at it backwards. The quills stick into the enemy's skin and break off, causing painful wounds.

rattling spines

stamping feet

There is more about hedgehogs on page 68.

Thematic links

Index of authors